THE *REAL* COWBOYS & ALIENS

UFO Encounters of the Old West

By
Noe Torres and John LeMay

Illustrated by
Jared Olive and Neil Riebe

RoswellBooks.com

Edinburg, Texas

ISBN: 978-1463748968

First Edition

Front Cover Illustration by Shane Olive

Chapter Heading Illustrations by Neil Riebe

Printed in the United States of America

To all the amazing monsters, fictional and otherwise, that gave us cold sweats and kept us awake at night as kids.

CONTENTS

INTRODUCTION

From the beginning of time, human beings have seen strange things in the sky. For example, the Bible tells the story of the prophet Ezekiel seeing an astonishing flying object landing and blasting off right in front of him. Several paintings of the Renaissance era clearly show flying saucers streaking across the sky. Also, ancient sea farers and explorers reported seeing UFOs hovering above them. Even the cowboys and ranchers of America's Old West occasionally witnessed strange flying objects.

Many people think that the flying saucer phenomena began in the 1940s. The idea that cowboys of the Old West may have encountered aliens seems very unlikely to them. Cowboys meeting aliens seems to be a theme strictly for comic books and blockbuster movies. But in reality, there exist many newspaper and magazine accounts from the 1800s telling of strange sightings and encounters from America's cowboy era. Included in these stories are sudden encounters with strange beings that were clearly not human.

What is especially interesting about these historic UFO sightings is that they took place before airplanes were invented and before manned flight was common. Although hot air balloons had been around since the 1700s, it was closer to 1900 before balloon airships became widely known.

Because airplanes and spaceships were unknown in the 1800s, people who saw strange things in the sky usually described them by comparing them to known objects like "cigars" and "balloons." The term "flying saucer" was not generally used for UFOs until the 1940s, but a Texas farmer who saw a UFO in 1878 described it as a "large saucer."

Since this was long before the era of jet planes and spacecraft, the cowboys and farmers of the 1800s often struggled to put into words what they had witnessed. Unless a UFO slowed down enough to where they could observe it carefully, most of the Old West residents probably didn't take much notice. Vapor trails in the daytime and streaks of light at night likely did not make much of an impression on these hardened pioneers. These sights were just part of the "signs and wonders" that often appeared in the heavens.

Although few records of these unexplained sightings exist, it seems likely that UFOs were quite common in the 1800s. We have found hundreds of newspaper and magazine accounts about people seeing strange objects and lights in the sky. We have also found articles that mention face-to-face encounters with creatures that seemed human but were clearly not.

In the pages ahead, you will read many bizarre stories, such as the one about a man from outer space whose spaceship crashed in North Texas and whose body was buried in a lonely Texas cemetery where it may still remain today. You will also read about a flying monster shot by two cowboys outside of Tombstone, Arizona. There is also a tale about an underwater UFO that came up to the surface and nearly electrocuted two men. Another story tells of a mysterious "airship" that lassoed a calf and then flew off into the sky with it. You will also hear the tale of a strange flying beast that terrorized a small Midwest town. Did these strange encounters really happen as recorded, or were they the products of overworked imaginations? We'll let you, our readers, decide for yourselves ...

CHAPTER 1
ROCKY MOUNTAIN UFO
EXPLOSION (1864)

The Rocky Mountains are a huge mountain range that stretches more than 3,000 miles from Canada all the way to faraway New Mexico. The Rockies play an important role in many Old West stories and legends. The Rockies were home to many Native American tribes and to the "Mountain Men," true pioneers of the Old West who braved nature's elements to survive. Many of these men were fur trappers who dedicated

4

themselves to catching animals like beavers so that they could sell their fur. It is with a fur trapper that we start our look at UFO encounters in the Old West.

James Lumley was a fur trapper in Montana, who witnessed what many people now believe was the crash landing of a UFO in the Rocky Mountains. What he experienced is one of the most interesting UFO cases of the 1800s.

In September 1864, Lumley was high in the mountains, trapping in an area known as Cadotte Pass. One night, after the sun had gone down, he saw a bright object streak through the sky. A newspaper article that appeared later in the *Cincinnati Commercial* described the object as a "bright, luminous body in the heavens, which was moving with a great rapidity in an easterly direction."

About five seconds after Lumley spotted it, the large object in the sky split into several smaller pieces with a flash like a "sky-rocket." Is it possible that the large object was a "mother ship" and that several smaller scout ships were expelled from it to the Earth below?

Moments later, Lumley heard and felt a tremendous explosion that shook the ground below his feet. This was followed by an eerie wind that swept through the forest with a loud rushing sound. There was also the

Typical Egyptian Heiroglyphics (Wikipedia)

distinctive smell of sulfur in the air, as when gunpowder is lit.

The newspaper said, "A few minutes later he heard a heavy explosion, which jarred the earth very perceptibly, and this was shortly after followed by a rumbling sound, like a tornado sweeping through the forest. A strong wind sprang up about the same time, but as suddenly subsided. The air was also filled with a peculiar odor of a sulphurous character."

The next morning, Lumley went to investigate. What he found was astonishing. Two miles from his camp, as far as the eye could see, was a wide path of destruction. "A path had been cut through the forest, several rods wide – giant trees uprooted or broken off near the ground - the tops of hills shaved off, and the earth plowed up in many places. Great and widespread havoc was everywhere visible." Lumley followed the trail of destruction until finally he found the mysterious object he had seen explode the night before. Embedded in the side of a mountain was what he described as "an immense stone."

It was soon clear that the object was not a fallen meteor. Lumley claimed that it was "divided into compartments" and parts of it had been "carved" with hieroglyphics, similar to the writings of ancient Egypt. The newspaper said, "He [Lumley] is confident that the hieroglyphics were the work of human hands, and that the stone itself, although but a fragment of an immense body, must have been used for some purpose by animated beings." Interestingly, strange writing that looks like hieroglyphics is seen very often in UFO cases. This was one of the very first cases where such mysterious writing is said to have been seen by an observer at the scene of a crashed UFO.

Lumley also found, littered around the site, fragments of glass. In addition, the ground around the crashed object was stained with some type of mysterious liquid. Maybe it was some kind of fuel that had leaked from the ship's engines?

The newspaper article went on to say, "Strange as this story appears, Mr. Lumley relates it with so much sincerity that we are forced to accept it as true." The article also mentions several other sightings of similar objects in the same time period, including another case where a large object split into several smaller ones.

The newspaper continued, "Astronomers have long held that it is probable that the heavenly bodies are inhabited -- even the comets -- and it may be that the

A STRANGE STORY—REMARKABLE DISCOVERY.—
Mr. James Lumley, an old Rocky Mountain trapper, who has been stopping at the Everett House for
several days, makes a most remarkable statement
to us, and one which, if authenticated, will pro-
duce the greatest excitement in the scientific world.

Mr. Lumley states that about the middle of last
September he was engaged in trapping in the mountains, about seventy-five or one hundred miles above
the Great Falls of the Upper Missouri, and in the
neighborhood of what is known as Cadotte Pass.
Just after sunset one evening he beheld a bright luminous body in the heavens, which was moving
with great rapidity in an easterly direction. It was
plainly visible for at least five seconds, when it suddenly separated into particles, resembling, as Mr.
Lumley describes it, the bursting of a sky-rocket
in the air. A few minutes later he heard a heavy

Portion of the Newspaper Article Published in 1865

meteors are also. Possibly, meteors could be used as a
means of conveyance by the inhabitants of other planets, in exploring space, and it may be that hereafter
some future Columbus, from Mercury or Uranus, may
land on this planet by means of a meteoric conveyance,
and take full possession thereof -- as did the Spanish
navigators of the New World in 1492, and eventually
drive what is known as the human race into a condition
of the most abject servitude. It has always been a favo-
rite theory with many that there must be a race superior
to us, and this may at some future time be demonstrated
in the manner we have indicated."

So what is one to make of James Lumley's mysterious space stone? Interestingly, in the first major
novel about an alien invasion of Earth, H. G. Wells'

The War of the Worlds (1898), the first alien spaceship that arrives is mistaken for a meteor. Its exterior is encrusted with dirt and rocks. Only when the aliens inside it began to unscrew the lid did the humans realize that the object was an artificial cylinder.

Even our own spacecraft, when they return to Earth, are often burned and distorted by their journey through the atmosphere. Is it possible then that what Lumley saw was a spaceship? Or was it merely a very strange rock from outer space that somehow became etched with markings that looked like hieroglyphics?

The mystery remains .....

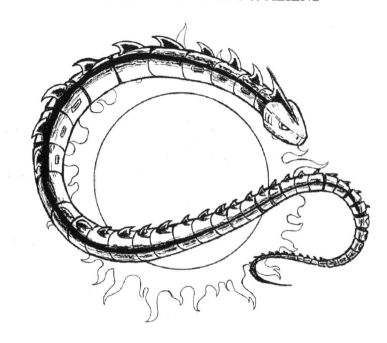

CHAPTER 2
THE FLYING SERPENT (1873)

Before airplanes were invented, people who saw UFOs often described them in strange ways. Sometimes they compared what they saw to an animal. For example, they might refer to them as giant birds or flying serpents.

At sunrise on June 26, 1873, residents of Fort Scott, Kansas, reported seeing what looked like a "huge serpent" encircling the sun. They saw the object when the sun was about halfway above the horizon. It remained visible "for some moments."

THE FLYING SERPENT (1873)

Image of Flying Serpent from 1589

The incident was printed in the local newspaper, the *Fort Scott Monitor*, on the following day, June 27. According to the newspaper, the sighting was reported by two very reliable witnesses. The witnesses were willing to sign sworn statements that they actually saw the flying serpent. The apparition was also seen by several soldiers of the U.S. Cavalry, who were stationed in Fort Scott.

Also in June 1873, at about the same time, something very similar was seen by a farmer named Mr. Hardin, who lived a few miles east of Bonham, Texas. A serpent-like object appeared in the sky above where Hardin was working. It was also seen by several other workers who standing in nearby fields. What they saw was unusual indeed, and the farmers became "seriously frightened," according to the local newspaper.

They described what they saw as an "enormous serpent" that seemed to float upon a cloud. "It seemed to be as large and as long as a telegraph pole, was of a yellow striped color, and seemed to float along without effort," the newspaper reported.

As the farmers continued to watch, the giant snake seemed to drift off toward the east. As it moved along in the sky, the serpent seemed to behave just like a real snake does. It would coil itself up, turn over, and thrust its head forward just like a snake does when it is about to bite.

The witnesses stated that the flying snake would "thrust forward its huge head as if striking at something, displaying the maneuvers of a genuine snake."

In his 1950 book *The Flying Saucers Are Real*, Donald Keyhoe argued that the sky serpent over Bonham was actually a flying saucer. Keyhoe wrote, "It was broad daylight when a strange, fast-moving object appeared in the sky, southwest of the town. For a moment, the people of Bonham stared at the thing, not believing their eyes. The only flying device then known was the drifting balloon. But this thing was tremendous and speeding so fast its outlines were almost a blur."

According to Keyhoe, terrified farmers hid under their wagons and townspeople fled indoors. Only a few people remained outdoors to view the object. The UFO circled the town twice before moving off to the east and disappearing.

The sighting appeared in the *New York Times*, but the story about it poked fun at the witnesses. The New York newspaper said that the farmers who claimed to see the flying serpent must have been delirious.

The *New York Times* also commented about the flying serpent seen in the skies over Fort Scott, Kansas. The writer said that if people continued to see flying snakes, the nation should consider banning the sale of alcoholic drinks.

Some years before these two cases, back in 1857 and 1858, settlers in Nebraska claimed to have also seen a huge flying serpent. Historian Mari Sandoz said that the creature was seen hovering in the sky over a steamboat. The serpent, which appeared to be "wavy," slipped in and out of the clouds. It also seemed to breathe fire and had streaks of light coming out of its sides.

The sighting in Nebraska was later put in a folk-song. The song describes the serpent as a "flyin' engine / Without no wing or wheel / It came a-roarin' in the

Aztec Sculpture of the feathered serpent god Quetzalcoatl (Courtesy of Neil Henderson, Wikimedia)

sky / With lights along the side / And scales like a serpent's hide." To some people, this sounds more like a flying saucer than a living creature.

Flying objects described as "flying serpents" have been seen throughout human history. For example, even the Bible mentions a "fiery flying serpent" (Isaiah 30:6). Paintings and sculptures of flying serpents have been found among artifacts of very ancient cultures, such as the Chinese, Maya, and Aztecs.

The feathered serpent god Quetzalcoatl was a most important part of Aztec religious beliefs.

The June 1873 incidents remain very interesting for a number of reasons. First, the witnesses seem believable. Second, the descriptions of both events were very similar.

What exactly was it that they saw in the sky? Was it really a snake-like creature or was it some kind of spacecraft that looked like a serpent?

CHAPTER 3

THE FARMER AND THE FLYING SAUCER (1878)

Strange flying ships seen in the sky were first called "flying saucers" in the late 1940s. But, long before that, back in 1878, a farmer in North Texas saw something in the sky that he described as a "a large saucer." It was the first time in history that the word "saucer" was used for a UFO.

The farmer, John Martin, was hunting on his property near Dallas, Texas. It was morning on Wednesday,

January 2, 1878. Suddenly, Martin noticed a dark object in the sky to the south.

When the farmer first saw it, the UFO was about the size of an orange. But, it grew in size rapidly as it approached his position. The local newspaper said, "The peculiar shape and velocity with which the object seemed to approach riveted his attention and he strained his eyes to discover its character."

Since it was morning and yet the object looked dark, it seems that the UFO did not have any lights. Instead, it appeared as a dark shape against the bright blue of the sky. Martin kept staring at it as it moved rapidly toward him. Martin said the UFO "appeared to be going through space at wonderful speed."

The brightness of the sky temporarily blinded Martin, and he lost track of where the object was. He rested

Daylight Disc Sighting in 1927 (Courtesy of UFOcasebook.com)

his eyes for a few moments. By the time he could see again, the UFO was right on top of him, and it was much larger than before.

The newspaper article said, "When directly over him it was about the size of a large saucer and was evidently at great height." So, although it was huge in size, it was also very high up in the sky. This means its true size was even larger than what it seemed to be.

Martin described the shape of the object as sort of like a balloon. But, although hot-air balloons already existed, they were extremely rare, and they did not move very fast.

Martin kept watching the UFO until it moved completely out of view. "It went as rapidly as it had come and was soon lost to sight in the heavenly skies," the newspaper said.

A report about the sighting appeared in the *Denison Daily News* on January 25, 1878. It was titled "A Strange Phenomenon" and consisted of a first-hand report from the farmer.

The newspaper article confirmed that Martin was a very trustworthy person. He was not the kind of person who would make up a false story. "Mr. Martin is a gentleman of undoubted veracity and this strange occurrence, if it was not a balloon, deserves the attention of our scientists," the article said.

In the book *Texas UFO Tales*, authors Mike Cox and Renee Roderick said that the UFO incident may have happened closer to Dallas than Denison, which is 72 miles north of Dallas. The authors said that Martin's story may have first appeared in the *Dallas Herald*. It was then picked up and republished by the newspaper

J. Allen Hynek (U.S. Government Photo)

in Denison.

In the early 1970s, Dr. J. Allen Hynek, a famous astronomer and UFO investigator, studied the Martin sighting. Hynek classified the incident as a "daylight disc." These types of UFOs usually travel very fast and make almost no sound. They sometimes make sudden, sharp turns while traveling extremely fast.

Daylight discs are often described as shiny or metallic. They usually display no lights. Sometimes, witnesses may hear a very faint "swishing" sound.

Daylight discs were mostly reported after 1940. So, this very unusual case from 1878 is extremely rare. It remains one of the most interesting UFO cases of the 1800s.

CHAPTER 4
THE GHOST LIGHTS OF MARFA, TEXAS (1883)

When something strange appears in the sky, like a UFO, it rarely happens on a regular schedule. Usually, there is a lot of luck involved in seeing something out of the ordinary. The witness just happens to be at the right place at the right time. However, in West Texas, there is a strange phenomenon that has been happening almost every night since the 1800s. It's called "The Marfa Lights."

The lights are brightly-glowing balls of fire that float and dance along the horizon every night beginning at around sundown. These "orbs" of light will suddenly sputter to life, like someone lighting a camp-

Photo of the Marfa Lights by Noe Torres

fire. They will sparkle and grow brighter, float around, move left and right, move up and down, and then suddenly, will grow dim and go out.

This apparition is hard to explain in words, but most people who actually see the lights are amazed and thrilled by them. That is why the State of Texas has built a special "Marfa Lights Viewing Area." The site has bathrooms and pay telescopes for viewing the lights. It is located on U.S. Highway 90, about nine miles east of Marfa, Texas. In order to see the lights, spectators look off to the southwest, toward the Chinati Mountains, and wait for them to appear.

Almost every night of the year, the viewing area fills up with curious people hoping to catch a glimpse of these mysterious lights. Getting a good view of the lights often depends on the weather, cloud conditions, and so on. The lights seem more "active" on certain nights, and there seem to be more lights appearing on some nights than on others.

Some people have associated the mysterious lights with UFOs. A number of UFO sightings have been recorded in the Marfa area over the years. A reported mid-air collision between a small plane and a UFO occurred in 1974, about 30 miles from where the lights are seen. The incident is known as "Mexico's Roswell."

For many years, investigators have tried to explain the Marfa Lights. Some people say they are headlights from cars traveling on a nearby highway. Other people say they are balls of gas or electrical energy. Still others say they are some form of geothermal energy that is escaping from the Earth's core.

The first serious attempt to discover their mystery came in the late 1800s. A railroad engineer named Walter T. Harris used surveyor's methods to find the exact location of the strange lights. He was not successful and concluded that the lights might be coming from deep within Mexico.

Over the decades, people have chased them. Airplanes have followed them. Scientists have studied them. Television programs have been done about them. Books have been written about them. And still, nobody knows for sure what they are. They remain one of Texas' most enduring and fascinating mysteries.

So, let's go back in time to one of the very first sightings ever recorded of the Marfa Lights. The time was 1883, and Texas was very much a dusty, frontier territory. Few people lived around Marfa, Texas.

A cowboy named Robert Reed Ellison and several other men had been herding cattle through the area around Marfa, Texas. On their second night in the area, they camped at a place called Paisano Pass. Suddenly, Ellison saw flickering lights in the distance and thought they were campfires lit by Apache Indians. Scrambling onto their horses, Ellison and his men went out into the desert, looking for the source of the mysterious lights.

For hours, the men searched along the base of the Chinati Mountains and in the mesa between their camp and where the lights had been. They saw no evidence that Indians had been anywhere in the area. They found no tracks, no doused campfires, and no other clues. Ellison was extremely puzzled and began to think that the lights were something very unusual.

For the next two nights, Ellison and his men again saw the strange lights. They were never able to solve the mystery, though.

Later, Ellison talked to local residents about what he had seen. They told him that many local people saw the lights frequently. Sometimes, people would wander out into the desert trying to find the lights or evidence about the lights, such as ashes that indicated a camp-

Chinati Mountain Range Near Marfa, Texas (Photo by Noe Torres)

fire. But, nobody had ever found any trace of what might cause the lights.

It seems likely that the lights were seen even before 1883. Historical accounts show that strange lights in the sky were seen by people riding on wagon trains from Ojinaga, Mexico, to San Antonio, Texas, back in the 1840s.

There is even a legend that says the lights are the ghost of a notorious Native American Chief named Alsate, who lived in the mid-1800s. Alsate grew up in Mexico, across the Rio Grande River from Lajitas, Texas. He was of the Mescalero Apaches and became a powerful and greatly feared war chief of the tribe. Alsate and his warriors went on frequent raids into Mexico, which caused the government to hunt him down.

The Mexican authorities eventually captured Alsate, executed him near Presidio, Texas, and then scattered his remaining followers, selling them into slavery throughout Mexico. After the chief's death, stories were told about his ghost being seen in the mountainous areas around Marfa, Texas, where the tribe used to camp. According to this legend, the mysterious Marfa Lights are also part of Alsate's ghostly apparitions.

In part because of this legend, the nearby Chinati Mountains are called the Ghost Mountains, and the strange lights are often called the Marfa "ghost lights." This incredible story is just another part of the continuing mystery of the Marfa Lights.

CHAPTER 5

THE COWBOYS SAW A UFO CRASH
(1884)

On Friday, June 6, 1884, a very strange thing happened while John W. Ellis and three other cowboys were rounding up cattle on a remote ranch about 35 miles northwest of Benkelman, Nebraska. The cowboys said they saw a flying saucer crash in a nearby ravine. The incident was reported in two separate newspapers of that time, the *Nebraska Nugget* and the *Daily State Journal* of Lincoln, Nebraska. About the area where it happened, the *Nugget* reported, "The country in the vicinity is rather wild and rough, and the roads are hardly more than trails."

The cattle roundup was suddenly interrupted when the three cowboys heard "a terrific whirring noise" in the sky above them. Looking up, they saw a blazing streak of light shooting down toward the ground. The witnesses later described it as a cylindrical airship, about 50 or 60 feet long and about 10 or 12 feet wide. It was composed of a strange metal that they later found to be extremely light.

The fiery cylinder struck the earth some distance away from where the cowboys stood. They could not see exactly where it had crashed, because it had fallen into a deep ravine.

The *Daily State Journal* later reported, "John W. Ellis, a well known ranchman, was going out to his herd in company with three of his herders and several other cowboys engaged in the annual roundup. While riding along a draw they heard a terrific rushing, roaring sound overhead, and looking up, saw what appeared to be a blazing meteor of immense size falling at an angle to the earth. A moment later it struck the ground out of sight over the bank."

Ellis and the others turned their horses and set off in search of the crash site. Moments later, they found it. According to the *Nebraska Nugget* newspaper of that time, the cowboys saw wreckage of a very strange appearance.

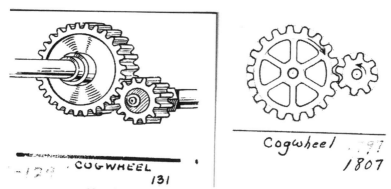

Sketches of Cogwheels (Courtesy of Wikimedia)

The newspaper said, "He [Ellis] rode at once to the spot, and it is asserted, saw fragments of cog-wheels, and other pieces of machinery lying on the ground, scattered in the path made by the aerial visitor, glowing with heat so intense as to scorch the grass for a long distance around each fragment and made it impossible for one to approach it."

Although "cog-wheels" makes it sound like an ordinary machinery, the witnesses may not have known how to describe it more exactly. They probably were just using images and words with which they were familiar.

More description was given about the wreckage: "One piece that looked like the blade of a propeller screw of a metal of an appearance like brass, about sixteen inches wide, three inches thick and three and a half feet long, was picked up by a spade. It would not weigh more than five pounds, but appeared as strong and compact as any known metal. A fragment of a wheel with a milled rim, apparently having had a diameter of seven or eight feet, was also picked up. It seemed to be of the same material and had the same remarkable lightness.

Interestingly, other reported UFO crashes that happened many decades later often included descriptions of extremely light metals. For example, in the alleged 1947 crash of a UFO near Roswell, New Mexico, witnesses claimed to see pieces of a metal that was very light and flexible but also very strong.

After witnessing the crash, the three cowboys approached the still-burning object. "Coming to the edge of the deep ravine into which the strange object had fallen, they undertook to see what it was. But the heat was so great that the air about it was fairly ablaze and it emitted a light so dazzling that the eye could not rest upon it more than a moment."

One of the cowboys, whose name was given as Alf Williamson, dismounted and approached the crashed UFO. Approaching to within 200 feet of the blazing wreckage, Williamson stuck his head over the edge of the ravine. Within 30 seconds, he "fell senseless from gazing at it at too close quarters." His hair was "singed to a crisp" and his face was covered with blisters.

The injured man was dragged away from the intensely hot area and taken to John W. Ellis' house, where he was cared for until a doctor could arrive to treat his wounds. His condition was said to be serious, and his brother, who lived in Denver, was summoned by telegraph.

This is one of the first accounts of a person being harmed during a UFO encounter. Although the injuries were described as heat-related, it's possible that radiation was also involved. Some of the people who

Library of Congress Photo of Nebraska Cattle Drive (LC-USF34- 008808-D)

Cylindrical Airship Design (NASA Photo)

approached the wreckage may have later suffered radiation-related illnesses and possibly death.

Examining the crashed object from a safe distance,

the remaining cowboys noticed that the ground around the UFO had been strangely affected by the crash. The newspaper said, "When it first touched the earth the ground was sandy and bare of grass. The sand was fused to an unknown depth over a space about 20 feet wide by 30 feet long, and the melted stuff was still bubbling and hissing. Between this and the final resting place there were several other like spots where it had come in contact with the ground, but no so well marked."

The only air travel known in 1884 was in hot air balloons, which had no engines and few mechanical parts. It is doubtful that the crash of a balloon could have caused such intense heat or radiation. It is also doubtful that it would have scattered so many strange pieces of metallic machinery all over the crash site.

Another interesting feature of the crashed object was an intense light that continued shining long after the crash. After nightfall, many people from neighboring ranches came to the crash site to view the mysterious object. But, even hours after it fell, the light was still too bright to look at directly. "The light emitted from it was like the blazing rays of the sun and too powerful to be borne by human eyes," the newspaper said.

On the following morning, June 7, 1884, the crash site was again visited by many of the local people. Among the visitors was E. W. Rawlings, an inspector of cattle brands for the local ranches. The wreckage had, by then, cooled a bit, although it was still too hot to touch.

After looking over the crash site, Rawlings went into the nearby town of Benkelman, Nebraska, and he supposedly verified that everything Ellis and the other cowboys had reported was true. The newspaper reported, "Great excitement exists in the vicinity and the roundup is suspended while the cowboys wait for the wonderful find to cool off so they can examine it. Mr. Ellis will go to the land office to secure the land on which the strange thing lies so that his claim to it cannot be disputed."

So, what finally happened to all the debris from this airship crash? In its June 10, 1884 edition, the *Daily State Journal* said, "It is gone, dissolved into the air. A tremendous rain storm fell yesterday afternoon beginning around 2 o'clock. As it approached, in regular blizzard style, most of those assembled to watch the mysterious visitor fled to shelter, a dozen or more, among them your correspondent, waited to see the effect of rain upon the glowing mass of metal. The storm came down from the north, on its crest a sheet of flying spray and a torrent of rain. It was impossible to see more than a rod through the driving, blinding mass. It lasted for half an hour, and when it slackened so that the aerolite should have been visible it was no longer there. The draw was running three feet deep in water and supposing it had floated off the strange vessel the party crossed over at the risk of their lives.

"They were astounded to see that the queer object had melted, dissolved by the water like a spoonful of salt. Scarcely a vestige of it remained. Small, jelly-like pools stood here and there on the ground, but under the eyes of the observers these grew thinner and thinner till they were but muddy water joining the rills that led to the current a few feet away. The air was filled with a faint, sweetish smell."

Skeptics insist that this UFO crash is false because one of the witnesses said that the wreckage included "fragments of cog- wheels," which were common pieces of machinery in the 19th century. However, as we have previously noted, just because he said it looked like cogwheels doesn't mean that they really were cogwheels. He may have just had no other way to describe it.

In the end, the only thing that can be said is what one of the newspaper articles from 1884 said, "The whole affair is bewildering to the highest degree, and will no doubt forever be a mystery."

CHAPTER 6
BIGFOOT FROM OUTER SPACE
(1888)

In the world of unexplained phenomena the big three are undoubtedly UFOs, the Loch Ness Monster and Bigfoot. Not surprisingly, due to its strange appearance, some people believe that Bigfoot is a hairy monster from another planet, dropped off on earth by a flying saucer.

The idea that Bigfoot and UFOs are connected is actually not something new. The first story suggesting

Bigfoot was a hairy castoff from a UFO appeared the late 1800s.

People in the Old West, especially Native Americans, reported seeing these large man-like beasts. Almost all Native Americans had legends of hairy giants resembling Bigfoot. Some tales were stranger than others and some even suggested that Bigfoot was a meat-eating cannibal!

The strangest Bigfoot story of all comes from a journal written by a Mr. Wyatt, a cattleman in California in the 1800s. The incident happened in 1888 in Humboldt County in the "Big Woods Country," where Wyatt had spent the winter with a Native American tribe. Wyatt had learned to speak the tribe's language and, having gained their trust, was allowed to participate in tribal activities.

One day, while out in the woods, Wyatt came across a local tribesman carrying a platter of raw meat. Wondering what was going on, and who the meat was for, Wyatt began to question the man. Although reluctant at first, the tribesman finally allowed Wyatt to follow him to a nearby shallow cave along a cliff face.

Inside the mysterious cave, a very strange creature sat cross-legged on the floor. The being looked like a man, except that it was very large, muscular and hairy. The man-beast was entirely covered in long, shiny, black hair, except for its palms and an area around its eyes. Also, the creature seemed to have no neck, its head appearing to rest directly upon its shoulders.

Despite its frightening appearance, the monster did not seem aggressive or dangerous. As Wyatt and the Native American approached, the creature sat contentedly, eating his meat. In fact, Wyatt said he went back to visit the creature on more than a dozen occasions. Unfortunately, Wyatt's diary gives no details of his other visits and does not say if he ever tried to communicate with the creature in any way. Curious about the man-beast, Wyatt asked the tribesmen questions about their mysterious "guest." Finally, after trading one man two pounds of tobacco, an axe and a compass, one of the tribesmen relented and told Wyatt the origin of their hairy visitor.

The tribesman took Wyatt to a high rock pinnacle and told Wyatt that men came down from the sky in "a small moon" and dropped off several hairy creatures, which the natives called "Crazy Bears," to the earth. The tribesman said this had happened several times before in the past.

He also said that men from the small moon looked like normal human beings, but they had short hair and wore tight-fitting, silver clothing. According to the tribesman, the men even waved to the humans in a friendly manner before closing the door to their spaceship and flying away!

After the "Crazy Bears" were dropped off, the Indians would round them up and escort them through their village. The locals at the time believed that the Crazy Bears were capable of "powerful medicine," which is why they fed and cared for them in the nearby caves. The tribesman apparently never told Wyatt what happened to all the other Crazy Bears that had been dropped off in the past, as he only saw one such creature during his time with the tribe.

Why would aliens drop off these Bigfoot creatures

Artist's Conception by Jared Olive

on the earth? Wyatt's grandson, James Wyatt, told paranormal investigator Brad Steiger that the aliens may have been conducting some sort of experiment.

Many people believe that Bigfoot may be the descendant of an extinct species of giant ape called *Gigantopithecus*, which stood nine feet tall and was covered in a thick layer of hair. If the Crazy Bears were descended from these ancient apes, perhaps they originated on Earth and not in outer space. Or maybe the visitors who rode the "small moons" picked up the apes, experimented on them, and then returned them to the Earth in a genetically-altered condition.

The story of the Crazy Bears isn't the only one to associate Bigfoot with UFOs. Many other Bigfoot

sightings have occurred at the same places and times that UFOs were spotted. Some witnesses have even claimed to have seen a Bigfoot creature vanish into thin air, as if it had stepped into another dimension. Perhaps this is why a Bigfoot has never been captured in the wild. The photo shown on the left is of a statue of Bigfoot at Klamath National Forest in California. It is courtesy of Barbara Torres and the U.S. National Park Service.

If the story told in Wyatt's diary is true, then perhaps Bigfoot really does come from outer space. It is certainly noteworthy that in many cases, Bigfoot-type creatures have been seen loitering around the area of a significant UFO sighting. In any case, the Crazy Bears story is one of the Old West's most interesting tales concerning UFOs and mysterious creatures.

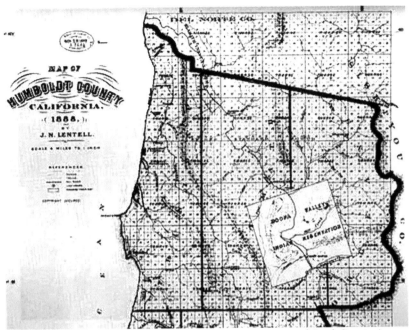

1888 Map of Humboldt County, California (National Park Service)

CHAPTER 7

THE PTERODACTYL THAT
TERRORIZED TOMBSTONE (1890)

Judging by the title of this chapter, you may be wondering what it's doing in a book about UFOs. After all, doesn't the word UFO always refer to a flying saucer? It is true that most UFOs are always thought to be flying saucers or other types of mystery craft, but technically a UFO can be any sort of unknown flying object. Anything you see in the sky and cannot identify can be considered a UFO.

What two cowboys saw outside of Tombstone, Arizona, one day back in 1890 might be called a PFO, or

38

Prehistoric Flying Object.

Tombstone had been made famous back in 1881, during the famous Gunfight at the OK Corral where Lawman Wyatt Earp shot it out with various bad guys. The local newspaper was appropriately named the *Epitaph*, since an epitaph is what you call the writing on someone's gravestone. It was in the April 26, 1890, edition of the *Tombstone Epitaph* that the story of the Pterodactyl was reported.

The story goes that on April 20 of the same year two cowboys were riding through the Huachuca desert located between the Whetstone Mountains and the Huachuca Mountains outside of Tombstone. In the long lonely stretch of desert they came upon a weary traveler, or perhaps a weary monster we should say.

On the dusty earth was an exhausted creature with a huge pair of wings the *Epitaph* described as, "A winged monster, resembling a huge alligator with an extremely elongated tail and an immense pair of wings...The creature was evidently greatly exhausted by a long flight..."

The story continues that the startled monster leapt to the sky and the cowboys chased it across the desert in an exciting horseback chase. Eventually the monster tired again and fell to the ground. The two cowboys then used their Winchester rifles to shoot at the monster. The bullets seemed to have little effect and the monster turned on the men, snapping its long tooth-lined beak at them.

The men backed up their horses and kept their distance from the wounded animal. The *Epitaph* continues, "After a few well directed shots the monster partly

rolled over and remained motionless. The men cautiously approached with their horses snorting in terror and found that the creature was dead."

According to the article the two men measured the creature at 92 feet in length! It also said the monster had only two feet, and the head was eight feet long with strong jaws lined with sharp teeth. Because its wings were folded under its dead body, it was difficult to measure the wings, but the two cowpokes estimated them to be 160 feet from wingtip to wingtip!

They said the creature was completely featherless, and hairless for that matter, and the wings were made of a thick, nearly transparent membrane. The skin was very smooth and could be cut off easily, which is why the men sliced off one of the wing tips to take back to Tombstone with them.

The *Epitaph* concludes, "Late last night one of them arrived in this city for supplies and to make the necessary preparations to skin the creature, when the hide will be sent east for examination by the eminent scientists of the day. The finder returned early this morning accompanied by several prominent men who will endeavor to bring the strange creature to this city before it is mutilated."

But did the men ever succeed in their mission to bring the monster to Tombstone? Maybe and maybe not. There exists a similar story about a photograph being published in an Old West newspaper, possibly the *Epitaph* of six men standing side by side with outstretched arms. Behind them is a huge bird nailed to a wall, its monstrous wings outstretched and its head hanging limp. The monster all in all stretched out to about 36 feet.

There are two problems with this photograph though. It was supposedly published in 1886, four years before the story of the cowboys killing a winged monster in 1890. Second, no one is able to find this alleged photograph and researchers have been searching for years. Several researchers claimed to have seen the photograph at one time or another, and one researcher even claimed to possess a copy of the photo. Only he had loaned it to someone that never returned it.

However, don't get too excited if you search the internet for the photo and think you've found it. Many people aware of the so-called missing pterodactyl photo have attempted to recreate it, and some are quite convincing.

Does the fact that no one, including the modern day offices of the *Epitaph* can find the photo, mean that either story is a hoax? Not necessarily, while the *Epitaph* likely exaggerated the 1890 monster's 160-foot wingspan, that doesn't mean there's no truth to the story.

In 1910, a witness surfaced who claimed to know the two cowboys that shot the monster. Harry McClure was a young man when he lived in the town of Lordsburg, New Mexico, about 97 miles northeast of Tombstone. McClure had known the two ranchers who told him the *Epitaph* account was greatly exaggerated. In reality the monster's wingspan was a more realistic (for a pterodactyl anyway) 20-30 feet. Further, the ranchers said the monster's two legs were horse-like, and it had large bulging eyes. Nor did they kill it, their bullets had little effect. The monster was able to fly away from them twice. The second time they let it go on its way, wherever that was.

But from where would such a creature have come? Coincidentally, Lordsburg, New Mexico, is a hotspot for UFO activity. Residents there claim that there is a portal in the sky they call the "Lordsburg Door" that UFOs fly out of. Some suspect the UFOs are really airplanes from the future, involving some sort of time travel. Presuming the Lordsburg Door might be some sort of time travel portal, did a dinosaur fly through the Lordsburg Door in the past only to be transferred to the future of the Wild West?

Probably not, but it is fun to speculate. There is another theory regarding where the monster came from. For years there had been a flying monster terrorizing people and animals in Lake Elizabeth, California. The flying monster was said to feed on chickens, cows and even horses!

The frustrated owner of the animals, Don Felipe Rivera, often shot his gun at the monster to little or no effect. It would simply fly into the air and then splash into the water where it would hide. Rivera's pterodactyl agitator was last seen in 1886, flying towards the East. Tombstone is east of California, which is why some speculate perhaps this was the same pterodactyl shot by the ranchers.

This story also isn't necessarily the only case of a living pterodactyl in the Old West. Most everyone has heard of the car the Thunderbird. But did you know where the car got its name? From a pterodactyl! Well, sort of. The Thunderbird was an animal said to exist by various Native American tribes across North America. It was a bird so huge it was said to be able to carry away men, and in one exaggerated story it picked a whale from the sea! One night the giant bird was struck by lightning, and the Indians therefore called it the Thunderbird.

Famous pioneer Daniel Boone even claimed to have once witnessed a Thunderbird carry away a five year old Indian boy. Boone says dozens of arrows were shot into the monster with no effect.

Some cryptozoologists, researchers and scientists that study monsters like Nessie (the Loch Ness Monster) and Bigfoot, now think the Thunderbird may have been a Pterodactyl or an extinct form of giant condor called the *Teratorn*.

CHAPTER 8

UFO EXPLODES OVER TEXAS COTTON GIN (1891)

In January 2008, several residents of Erath County in North Texas saw a huge UFO in the skies above them. The object, estimated to be about half a mile long, was seen near the towns of Stephenville, Texas, and Dublin, Texas. After this happened, some of the older residents remembered a UFO case that took place many years earlier, back in 1891. That was when a flying object exploded in the sky above a local cotton gin.

The UFO sighting took place on Saturday, June 13, 1891, a quiet summer day, in the small town of Dublin, Texas. At that time, the town had a population of about 2,000 people, and one of its major businesses was the Wasson & Miller flour mill and cotton gin.

Simulation of Explosion over Cotton Gin

The gin was closed for the weekend, and several towns-people were out for a walk near it when they suddenly noticed something very unusual in the sky above the gin. Witnesses saw a bright, oblong-shaped object hovering about 300 feet up.

An eyewitness, whose name was not given, told the local newspaper that what he saw looked like "a bale of cotton suspended in the air after having been saturated in kerosene oil and ignited, except that it created a much brighter light."

The witness said that the light was so bright it "dazzled" people who were standing several hundred feet away from the light. This is a mystery, since bright artificial lights did not exist in the year 1891. Although electric light bulbs had been invented a few years before, they were not widely available yet.

In the 1890s, the most common sources of light

were kerosene lamps and campfires. Neither of these was very bright.

Some people think that the brilliant light might have been caused by an electrical fire or explosion inside the UFO. Maybe the flying object had overheated, causing it to glow brightly before the whole thing blew up in the sky.

Although the local newspaper later described it as a "meteor," the UFO did not look or behave like a meteor. It seemed to "hover" over the gin, and it gave out an extremely intense light. Also, it shattered into pieces *before* it hit the ground.

The witness continued watching the bright light until the flying object suddenly exploded. After the explosion, chunks of a strange, burning-hot metal fell to the ground, setting the grass and weeds on fire. The explosion of the UFO was so loud that it was heard by "nearly everyone in that portion of the city," according to the newspaper.

The man who witnessed this event was so scared by what he saw that he ran away from the gin and hid himself. Later, when he was asked to provide the exact size and appearance of the UFO before it exploded, he could not. He said he was too scared to pay close attention.

After returning to his home, the witness continued thinking about the UFO and was not able to sleep well. He decided that he would return to the scene of the explosion early the next morning – Sunday, June 14, 1891.

The witness was embarrassed at having run away, and he wanted to conduct an investigation into what

The Old Cotton Gin (Right) As It Looks Today (Courtesy of Mark Murphy)

happened. When he went back, his eyes beheld an amazing sight. Scattered across a field of burned grass and weeds were strange pieces of metal. He described them as "fragments of the most remarkable substance ever known to explode." The metal was of the same color as lead. He also saw some "peculiar stones" that looked like lava from a volcano. And there was something else – even more mysterious. As the witness looked around, he found several small pieces of what looked like paper with strange writing on it.

It looked like torn pieces from a newspaper, but the writing on it was not English. In fact, nobody could identify what language it was. "The language … was entirely foreign to him, and, in fact, no one has yet been found who has ever seen such a language before," said the report about the incident, which appeared later in the *Dublin Progress*.

48

A Meteor Explodes in the City--An Eye
Witness Describes the Scene to a
Progress Reporter--Scared.

Quite a little excitement was created last Saturday night by the bursting of what is supposed by those who were present to have been a meteor, near Wasson & Miller's gin. Quite a number witnessed the explosion and nearly everyone in that portion of the city heard the report eminating therefrom, which is said to have sounded somewhat like the report of a bomb-shell. Our informant (who, though a little nervous at times, is a gentleman who usually tells the truth, but did not give us this statement with a view to its publication) says he observed the meteor when it was more than three hundred feet in the air, before bursting, and that it bore a striking resemblance to a bale of cotton suspended in the air after having been saturated in kerosene oil and ignited, except that it created a much brighter light, almost dazzling those who percieved it. The gentleman in question seems to have been so badly frightened that it was utterly impossible to obtain an accurate account of the dimensions and general appearance of this rare phenomenon, but we are convinced from his statements that his position at the time must have been very embarrassing and that very little time was spent in scientific investigations. However, on the following morning he returned to the scence so hastily left the previous night, to find the weeds,

grass, bushes and vegetation of every description for many yards around the scene of the explosion burned to a crisp, also discovering a number of peculiar stones and pieces of metal, all of a leaden color. presenting much the appearance of the lava thrown out by volcanic eruptions. He also picked up some small fragments of manuscript and a scrap, supposed to be part of a newspaper, but the language in both was entirely foreign to him, and, in fact, no one has yet been found who has ever seen such a language before, hence no information could be gained from their examination. At this juncture your reporter requested that he be shown these wonderful fragments of such a miraculous whole, but the narrator had worked himself up to such a pitch of excitement that it was impossible to get him to grasp the significance of our request, and were compelled to leave him a victim to his own bewildered fancy and to ruminate the seemingly miraculous story he had just related. Thus was a repotorial zealot denied the boon of seeing fragments of the most remarkable substance ever known to explode near Wasson & Miller's gin.

P. S. Since the above was put in type we learn that our reporter was given the above information by a contributor to the Dublin Telephone, but the information came too late to prevent its insertion in this paper.

Original Newspaper Article from 1891 (Courtesy of Mark Murphy)

After finding the scraps of paper with the strange writing, the witness became completely "bewildered." The newspaper reporter said that the witness "worked himself up to such a pitch of excitement" that he could not answer any more questions. He would not show any of the wreckage to the reporter or talk any more about it.

The cotton gin where the UFO exploded still exists today. The local museum in Dublin, Texas, hopes to restore the building and preserve it as a historical landmark. Dublin is well known in Texas as the town where the soft drink known as Dr. Pepper got its start. The very first Dr. Pepper bottling plant was built there in 1891.

Until now, nobody has tried to find any of the strange pieces of metal that fell to ground. Some of the fragments may still be there, buried under the surface. It is possible that someday, the material will be found. In addition, nobody has ever found traces of the paper with the strange writing on it. Maybe it still exists today in somebody's attic?

CHAPTER 9
THE CRAWFORDSVILLE FLYING MONSTER (1891)

Back in the 1800s, there weren't really any serious UFO researchers like there are today. One of the first men to take accounts of strange creatures and unidentified flying objects seriously was a man named Charles Fort.

Fort was born in 1874 and as an adult he began going through and collecting old newspaper articles from earlier days, specifically the strange ones. Fort eventually published his findings in several books. As a result people began to refer to strange things as "fortean events" after the famous researcher. In a similar manner are creatures called Fortean monsters, which are so strange looking they make Bigfoot and Nessie look downright normal in comparison.

One such Fortean Monster believed to possibly be from outer space researched by Fort was the flying monster of Crawfordsville. Fort read about the beast in the September 10, 1891 edition of the *Brooklyn Eagle*.

Fort was so perplexed by the creature's appearance that he assumed it to be a hoax. To see if this was the case or not, Fort wrote a letter to one of the witnesses of the monster mentioned in the newspaper. To Fort's surprise the man, Reverend G.W. Switzer, was a real person. While Fort proved that Switzer was real, he unfortunately could not do the same for the monster.

The story originally reported in the *Crawfordsville Journal* in early September of 1891 went like this:

It was midnight on Saturday, September 5, 1891, and Reverend G.W. Switzer of the First Methodist Church in Crawfordsville, Indiana, had gotten up to get some water from his well when he saw what was surely the strangest sight of his life.

Snaking through the air was an almost formless creature comprised of hundreds of white fluttering fins. Rev. Switzer awakened his wife who also got to see the creature which they both said was, "[swimming] through the air in a writhing, twisting manner similar to the glide of some serpents."

At one point the couple describes the monster as swooping so close to the ground that it nearly touched the lawn of Lane Place before it continued its flight over the town.

The good revered and his wife weren't the only ones to see the monster that night. So did two ice delivery men, Marshall McIntyre and Bill Gray, who had gotten up early to prepare their wagon for delivery rounds for later in the morning. It was about 2 o'clock in the morning as the two were preparing the wagon and all of a sudden a feeling of "awe and dread" overcame them.

Turning their heads to sky they saw a monster that they described as, "about eighteen feet long and eight feet wide and moved rapidly through the air by means of several pairs of side fins. . . . It was pure white and had no definite shape or form, resembling somewhat a great white shroud fitted with propelling fins. There was no tail or head visible but there was one great flaming eye, and a sort of a wheezing plaintive sound was emitted from a mouth which was invisible. It flapped like a flag in the winds as it came on and frequently gave a great squirm as though suffering unutterable agony."

The two men, who said the monster hovered about three to four hundred feet in the air, were able to observe the creature for a whole hour. Eventually the two got scared, harnessed their horses, and left the area.

The next morning, when the other townsfolk heard of the sightings they laughed at the witnesses and accused them of drinking, even the Reverend! Switzer was even sent an "invitation" to come to a clinic for people who abused alcohol.

Crawfordsville residents stopped laughing the next night when the monster was seen by nearly 100 townsfolk. They probably all looked to the sky that night out of curiosity, to see if they too would witness the monster. And so they did. At one point it was said the monster swooped close to the ground and the frightened onlookers could even feel its hot breath!

After that, the Crawfordsville Monster was never seen from again. The story soon went on the wires to many other newspapers, and soon after the Crawfordsville Postmaster soon found himself buried in mail regarding the monster. Some people thought the monster heralded the end of the world, and one woman thought the monster had also been seen in Chicago.

So just what was the Crawfordsville Monster? Most people today think the monster was an Atmospheric Beast—a sort of gaseous living organism. Famous scientist Carl Sagan even speculated such creatures could exist on gas planets like Jupiter.

A Fortean investigator living in Crawfordsville, Vincent P. Gaddis, did the more research on the monster than anyone and concluded, "All the reports refer to this object as a living thing -- in other words, one of the hypothetical atmospheric life forms that would figure in early theories about unidentified flying objects."

In the 1990s, a new type of mystery animal was introduced to the world – "rods." Rods are a small insect-like animal – basically like a stick bug with little fins

Artist's Conception by Jared Olive

along its sides - that quickly darts through the air. Most people see them on home video recordings and then use slow motion to get a clear look at the "monster." A recent episode of the History Channel's TV show *Monster Quest* theorized that perhaps the Crawfordsville Monster was a giant "rod."

Skeptics claim that on the night of the second major sighting in 1891, two Crawfordsville men followed the monster until they finally concluded that it was really a giant flock of birds! The two men, John Hornbeck and Abe Hernley, said the birds many wings accounted for the propelling fins, and the birds many shrieks accounted for the mysterious noise. The *Crawfordsville Journal* further speculated that low visibility in the damp night air caused the misidentification, and that newly installed electric lights in the town caused the birds to go crazy.

While it's tempting to shout, "Case Closed!" one must remember, while the birds' wings could explain the many "fins," what then would explain the single flaming eye? Otherworldly, indeed.

CHAPTER 10

THE UNDERWATER UFO (1893)

Almost everyone knows that UFO stands for Un-identified Flying Object. But did you also know there is such a thing as an Unidentified Submersible Object or USO? A USO is what people call an unidentified object that is seen in or under the water. There have actually been many USO encounters in the world since 1940. Even more surprising, there were also USO sightings during the Old West.

The most interesting USO encounter of the 1800s occurred near Tacoma, Washington on July 2, 1893. The story began on a Saturday afternoon (July 1) at about 4:30 when a group of "well-known gentlemen" departed Tacoma on a boat called *Marion* for a three-day fishing and hunting excursion. A newspaper article said, "The party consisted of Auctioneer William Fitzhenry, H.L. Seal, W.L. McDonald, J.K. Bell, Henry Blackwood and two eastern gentlemen who are visiting the coast."

After several hours of fishing on the Puget Sound, the men decided to go ashore at a place called Black Fish Bay on Henderson Island, where they would camp and spend the night. As it turned out, they made camp within 100 yards of a group of men who were engaged in surveying the area.

Around midnight, one of the fishermen awoke suddenly. He later told a local newspaper, "It was, I guess, about midnight before I fell asleep, but exactly how long I slept I cannot say, for when I woke it was with such startling suddenness that it never entered my mind to look at my watch, and when after a while I did look at my watch, as well as every watch belonging to the party, it was stopped."

He had been awakened by a very loud noise. "I was in the midst of a pleasant dream, when in an instant a most horrible noise rang out in the clear morning air, and instantly the whole air was filled with a strong current of electricity that caused every nerve in the body to sting with pain, and a light as bright as that created by the concentration of many arc lights kept constantly flashing."

Because of the loud noise and electric charge in the air, the witness thought that the fishermen were caught in the middle of an intense thunderstorm. But, looking up at the sky, he saw no evidence of lightning, and

1856 Illustration of a Sea Monster (Wikimedia)

instead, he noticed strange lights coming from the water of the nearby bay.

By now, the other fishermen and the surveyors were awake and could also see the disturbance occurring in the water. Approaching the shore towards the frightened group was what the witness later described as "a most horrible-looking monster."

The "monster fish," as they called it, was 150 feet long, but the description sounds more like a giant caterpillar than a fish. The beast had a head that resembled a walrus, but with six eyes the "size of dinner plates."

The witness also said, "At intervals of about every eight feet from its head to its tail a substance that had the appearance of a copper band encircled its body, and it was from these many bands that the powerful electric current appeared to come."

The bizarre creature also had two horn-like protrusions sticking from its head. Since the beast was caterpillar-like, perhaps they were antennae? Even stranger, these two "horns" were spraying water that looked like "blue fire" because of its electric charge.

The newspaper account said, "The monster slowly drew in toward the shore, and as it approached from its head poured out a stream of water that looked like blue fire. All the while the air seemed to be filled with electricity, and the sensation experienced was as if each man had on a suit of clothes formed of the fine points of needles. One of the men from the surveyor's camp incautiously took a few steps in the direction of the water, and so he did so the monster darted towards the shore and threw a stream of water that reached the man, and he instantly fell to the ground and lay as though dead."

A second man, Mr. McDonald, rushed to help the fallen surveyor, but he too was struck by the water and fell to the ground. "Mr. McDonald attempted to reach the man's body to pull it back to a place of safety, but he was struck with some of the water that the monster was throwing, and fell senseless to the earth. By this time every man in both parties was panic-stricken, and we rushed to the woods for a place of safety, leaving the fallen men lying on the beach."

Even from inside the protection of the trees, the men said they could see the monster's glow light up the sky, and its thunderous roar could be heard for miles around. Luckily for them, the monster never came ashore and instead changed course diving underneath the water. Although it was no longer on the surface, the men could still see the monster's glow as it traveled under the water. Eventually, its glow faded away, and the monster was never seen again.

Artist's Conception by Jared Olive

The men made their way back to their fallen companions. Luckily, the two men were not dead, just knocked unconscious by the mysterious water.

When asked for a detailed description of the monster, one of the witnesses said, "This monster fish, or whatever you may call it, was fully 150 feet long, and at its thickest part I should judge about thirty feet in circumference. Its shape was somewhat out of the ordinary in so far that the body was neither round nor flat but oval, and from what we could see the upper part of the body was covered with a very coarse hair.

"The head was shaped very much like the head of a

walrus, though, of course, very much larger. Its eyes, of which it apparently had six, were as large around as a dinner plate, and were exceedingly dull, and it was about the only spot on the monster that at one time or another was not illuminated.

"At intervals of about every eight feet from its head to its tail a substance that had the appearance of a copper band encircled its body and it was from these many bands that the powerful electric current appeared to come. The bands nearest the head seemed to have the strongest electric force, and it was from the first six bands that the most brilliant lights were emitted.

"Near the center of its head were two large horn-like substances, though they could not have been horns, for it was through them that the electrically charged water was thrown.

"Its tail from what I could see of it was shaped like a propeller, and seemed to revolve, and it may be possible that the strange monster pushes himself through the water by means of this propeller like tail."

While this mysterious apparition may seem more like a sea monster than an unidentified object, the "creature" seemed more machine than flesh and blood. As is the case with many Old West UFO sightings, the objects were often described using the characteristics of known animals, such as birds, fish, and insects. In this case, the strange object seemed to be in the shape of an animal, but it may well have been a mechanical device.

In support of the machine theory, witnesses said the monster's body was encircled by something that looked like copper wire. The witnesses also said the monster's tail was like the propeller, spinning round and round.

1869 Drawing of Jules Verne's Nautilus (Wikipedia)

Also, the six eyes, as large as dinner plates, could easily have been portholes, allowing the ship's occupants to see outside their vessel.

This amazing story was published in the *Tacoma Daily Ledger*, on July 3, 1893. It appears to have been based mainly on the testimony of one of the fishermen, whose name was not given. He was not identified, except to say that he was "from the East."

In the last mention of this mysterious eyewitness, the man told the newspaper, "I am going to send a full account of our encounter to the Smithsonian institute, and I doubt not but what they will send out some scientific chaps to investigate. Now I must be going, as I have to leave on tonight's train, but if you need any further particulars you can obtain them from any of the party. No, I do not know who composed the survey party; all I know about them is that they are from Olympia and that they were on the island running farm lines on some disputed land."

Although it remains a very intriguing account from the Old West, critics say that perhaps the witness made up the story for the amusement of their friends. Skeptics point out that sometimes, in the late 1800s, newspapers published wildly sensational stories in order to sell more newspapers. Some of these published stories were more legend than fact. Occasionally newspapers were even accused of publishing completely fake stories.

Interestingly, the famous Jules Verne novel, *Twenty Thousand Leagues under the Sea*, was published in French in 1869 and in English in 1873. The novel is about an eccentric inventor who builds the world's first submarine. To the sailors who see it, the vessel appears to be a huge sea monster.

So was the Tacoma USO a real mechanical monster, or was it a hoax that should have never been published as a true news story? Regardless of whether it is true or not, the story remains the 19th century's most fascinating account of an underwater submersible object.

CHAPTER 11
THE MYSTERIOUS AIRSHIPS OF 1896

As the 19th century was coming to an end, the world was changing. The time of the Old West was coming to an end. Railroads were opening up the entire country to settlement. Machines were being used more and more in business and industry. In 1896, automobiles, called "horseless carriages" were starting to become common. Telephone systems were expanding. Also in 1896, America's transcontinental railroad was completed, and the first x-ray machine was unveiled.

As far as air travel, hot-air balloons were in use in 1896. Also, experiments had begun on adding petroleum engines to balloons. But, engine-driven balloons did not become common until after 1900. Airplanes were born in 1903 after the Wright brothers made their successful test flights at Kitty Hawk.

But, before all this, in November 1896, people all over California and Washington State began seeing strange airships in the sky. Since most people had read about airships that several inventors were working on in Europe, the objects they saw in the sky were called "airships."

In reality, many of these objects were clearly not balloons at all. Many of them were metallic looking. Some were flat, instead of blimp-like. Some of them travelled much too fast to be balloons and made some very strange maneuvers. Also, in several cases, strange humanoid beings were seen in or around these ships. If these airships had been seen in our time, they would have been called unidentified flying objects.

The first documented sightings took place on several nights in November 1896 in Sacramento, California. Witnesses saw a strange, glowing light in the sky that appeared to be attached to the bottom of some sort of flying ship. People could not really make out any details about the ship itself, but the glowing light was very frightening to them. Newspaper headlines talked about the "mystic flying light" and the "phantom airship." Although the phenomenon was mainly observed in Northern California, occasionally, it was seen as far south as Los Angeles.

The November 22, 1896 edition of *The San Fran-*

65

The Mysterious Flying Light That Hovered Over St. Mary's College, Oakland, and Then Started for San Francisco. It Is Exactly Like That Described by Sacramentans, and Similar to the Cut Published a Few Days Ago in "The Call" From a Description Furnished by One Who Saw It.

Sketch Published in San Francisco newspaper, 11-22-1896

cisco Call quoted witnesses who said the UFO "appeared to descend gradually and regularly, as if under perfect control." One witness said, "There is no doubt in my mind that it was an airship supplied with electric lights and well-manned."

Especially interesting in the descriptions was the bright light at the bottom of the ship. It was pointed toward the earth below as the object coasted overhead. A witness said, "The machine was brilliantly lighted, and … the lower light shed a large arc on the ground as it passed over, while the headlight could be seen for a great distance ahead of the machine."

In many later sightings, such as in the 1950s and 1960s, UFOs were often observed shining a bright light down to the Earth below as they passed overhead. In some cases, light beams from a UFO were seen lighting up the entire landscape below for miles ahead of the ship.

Also on November 22, two Methodist ministers, Reverends H. Copeland and John Kirby, observed a red "fireball" with white lights on the front and back. They saw it near Knight's Ferry, California, about 40 miles east of Modesto. They watched as the UFO rose up into the air, then descend and skim along the ground, and finally disappear from sight.

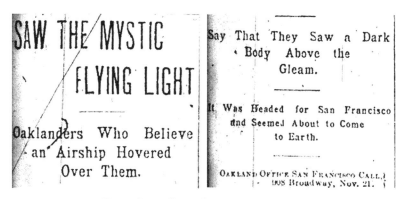

Typical Headlines during Airship Scare

But the most incredible of all the 1896 airship sightings came on November 25, near Lodi, California. While travelling in a horse-drawn carriage, Colonel H. G. Shaw and Mr. Camille Spooner saw three very tall beings standing alongside the road. In the distance behind them, a huge, cigar-shaped UFO hovered quietly over a body of water.

In an article in the *Stockton Evening Mail*, Colonel Shaw said, "Looking up we beheld three strange beings. They resembled humans in many respects, but

Artist's Conception (Wikimedia)

still they were not like anything I had ever seen... They were possessed of a strange and indescribable beauty." Shaw added that they wore no clothes, but their bodies were covered by soft, fine fuzz. "They were seven feet in height and very slender. I noticed, further, that their hands were quite small and delicate, and that their fingers were without nails. Their feet, however, were nearly twice as long as those of an ordinary man, though they were narrow, and the toes were also long and slender. I noticed, too, that they were able to use their feet and toes much the same as a monkey; in fact, they appeared to have much better use of their feet than their hands."

As for other features, Shaw said, "Their faces and heads were without hair, the ears were very small, and the nose had the appearance of polished ivory, while the eyes were large and lustrous. The mouth, however, was small, and it seemed to me that they were without teeth."

They were also extremely light. Shaw said, "As one of then came close to me I reached out to touch him, and placing my hand under his elbow pressed gently upward, and lo and behold I lifted him from the ground with scarcely an effort. I should judge that the specific gravity of the creature was less than an ounce."

Shaw attempted to communicate with the creatures. He said, "I asked where they were from. They seemed not to understand me, but began – well, 'warbling' expresses it better than talking. Their remarks, if such you would call them, were addressed to each other, and sounded like a monotonous chant, inclined to be guttural."

In addition, the beings used several strange tools, including what seemed to be a machine to help them breathe. Shaw said, "Each of them had swung under the left arm a bag to which was attached a nozzle, and every little while one or the other would place the nozzle on his mouth, at which time I heard a sound of escaping gas."

The beings also carried another tool that was a sort of lamp. "Each held to his hand something about the size of a hen's egg. Upon holding them up and partly opening the hand, these substances emitted the most remarkable, intense and penetrating light one can imagine. Notwithstanding its intensity it had no unpleasant effect upon our eyes, and we found we could gaze directly at it. It seemed to me to be some sort of luminous mineral, though they had complete control of it," Shaw said.

The strange beings seemed to make an attempt to "abduct" Colonel Shaw and Mr. Spooner. "One of them, at a signal from one who appeared to be the leader, attempted to lift me, probably with the intention of carrying me away. Although I made not the slightest resistance he could not move me, and finally the three of them tried it without the slightest success. They appeared to have no muscular power outside of being able to move their own limbs."

After the failed abduction attempt, the creatures moved toward a nearby canal. "There, resting in the air about twenty feet above the water was an immense airship," Shaw said. "It was 150 feet in length at least, though probably not over twenty feet in diameter at the widest part. It was pointed at both ends, and outside of a large rudder there was no visible machinery."

The beings seemed to glide as they went, sometimes not even touching the ground. Shaw said, "The three walked rapidly toward the ship, not as you or I walk, but with a swaying motion, their feet only touching the ground at intervals of about fifteen feet. We followed them as rapidly as possible, and reached the bridge as they were about to embark. With a little spring they rose to the machine, opened a door in the side, and disappeared within."

The ship then "went through the air very rapidly and expanded and contracted with a muscular motion, and was soon out of sight."

Airship sightings all across California continued through December 1896. Then, suddenly, as the year came to a close, no more were reported. The mysterious airship wave of 1896 had ended.

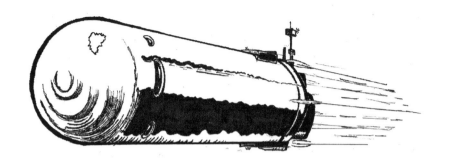

CHAPTER 12
THE SECOND AIRSHIP WAVE (1897)

After the California airship sightings ended in December 1896, several weeks went by without any more activity. But, beginning in late January and continuing through June of 1897, the United States was again gripped by "airship hysteria." Sightings of the strange ships broke out in Nebraska and pretty soon were seen all over the country.

While engine-driven balloon ships were already being developed, they were not yet being widely used. Most of the man-made dirigibles were still in the experimental stage. That's why many people believe that the airships seen all over the nation in 1897 were something mysterious and unexplained.

The wave of new sightings began in Hastings, Nebraska on January 25, 1897. Witnesses told the *Omaha Bee* newspaper that they had seen "a large, glaring light" moving at a "remarkable speed" about 500 feet above the ground. The newspaper said the light "was seen to circle around for a few minutes and then descended for about 200 feet, circling as it traveled at a remarkable speed for about two miles and then slowing up it circled for fully 15 minutes, when it began to lower and disappear as mysteriously as it had made its appearance."

The object was seen again just west of Hastings on January 31, hovering motionless in the sky about 800 feet in the air. The newspaper said, "At first sight it had the appearance of an immense star, but after closer observation the powerful light shows by its color to be artificial. It certainly must be illuminated by powerful electric dynamos for the light sent forth by it is wonderful."

Several days later, the object was seen again, this time about 40 miles to the south. The witnesses were returning home from a prayer meeting at church when they heard rumbling noises, strange voices, and even laughter from the air above them.

Looking up, they saw a very strange object. The February 5, 1897 edition of the *Omaha Bee* reported, "It seemed to be conical-shaped and perhaps 30 to 40 feet in length, with a bright headlight and six smaller lights, three on a side, and seemed to have two sets of wings on a side, with a large fan-shaped rudder."

The Nebraska sightings continued. On February 17, three men told the *Kearney Hub* newspaper that they saw a barrel-sized object rise suddenly up into the air about 300 feet before descending and shooting out sparks. A similar object was seen in North Loup on March 13.

Sketch from Chicago Times-Herald, 4-12-1897

In the days that followed, bright lights were seen in the skies over several Nebraska towns. Witnesses described what they saw as a "big searchlight" and a "big [train] engine headlight" in the sky.

Late in February and on into March, these mysterious luminous objects were also being seen in the neighboring state of Kansas. The *Kansas City Star* newspaper described a sighting where a UFO zoomed across the sky at 75 miles per hour and lit up parts of the town of Belleville, Kansas, "like an immense meteor." The object then came to a complete standstill in the sky for about 30 minutes before dancing around "playfully" and then zooming out of sight.

The March 29 edition of the *Kansas City Times* reported an object over Topeka, Kansas, that "moved parallel with the horizon with great rapidity." The newspaper noted that "stars do not perform these feats. Neither do planets."

By April 1897, the airship mystery had spread to many other states, including Illinois, Michigan, Iowa, Indiana, Ohio, and Texas. In some cases, the ships seen in the sky looked a lot like experimental engine-driven balloons. In other cases, the ships looked more like what we think of as UFOs.

One of the more impressive sightings occurred on the evening of April 10 in Quincy, Illinois. Hundreds of people saw an object between 50 and 100 feet in length with an intense white light and smaller colored lights. The object flew low across the city's west side, came to a full stop, and then reversed its course.

Man-made Airship of the 20th Century (Wikimedia)

The *Quincy Morning Whig* reported, "At times it did not appear to be more than 400 or 500 feet above the ground, and in the bright moonlight was plainly silhouetted against the clear sky. Men who saw the thing describe it as a long, slender body shaped like a cigar, and made of some bright metal, perhaps aluminum, on which the moonlight glistened. On either side of the hull extending outwards and upwards were what appeared to be wings, and above the hull could be seen the misty outlines of some sort of superstructure, a clear view of which, however, was intercepted by the wings. At the front end of the thing was a headlight, and from the brightness and intensity of the stream of light thrown out it was apparently similar to the searchlights used on steamboats. About midway of the hull were small lights, a green light on the starboard or right hand side, and a red light on the port or left hand side."

Airships of similar design were seen throughout the month of April in other parts of the Midwest and Northern states. The ships were typically described as cylindrical or cigar-shaped and often had bright lights on them and attachments that looked like "wings."

These bizarre airships were seen as far south as Texas. On April 15, the *Dallas Morning News* reported that an amateur astronomer, looking at the sky using powerful field glasses, had seen an object in Cresson, Texas, that "floated about a half mile above the earth and seemed to be about 50 feet long, of a cigar shape with two great wings thrust out from each side." The UFO also had "a powerful search light" that "threw its rays far into the night ahead, beside which even the luminosity of the moon paled."

Similar sightings in April occurred in Illinois, North Dakota, Indiana, Ohio, and other parts of Texas. Strangely, in some of the sightings, people on the ground heard voices coming from the airships. On April 11, at Hawarden, Iowa, as a 60-foot long airship passed overhead, witnesses heard "the sound of human voices ... among which was mingled the laughter of women."

Voices were also heard in a number of other sightings during April 1897. In almost every case, the language that was heard coming from the airships could not be understood. It did not seem to be English.

Additionally, witnesses sometimes claimed they saw people aboard the mysterious airships. On April 11 in Minnetonka, Minnesota, a ground observer said he saw inside an airship "living persons – men, women, and children. They were moving about as if very busy," according to the *Minneapolis Tribune*.

In some cases, witnesses would actually talk to some of the occupants of these airships. For example, an airship that was seen in many parts of Texas was supposedly piloted by a man who called himself "Mr. Wilson." Several people talked to Wilson during times when he would land his airship to get supplies. Wilson claimed to be an "inventor" from New York, but all attempts to locate information about him later were unsuccessful.

Other people encountered airship crews that did not seem quite human. On April 14, near Reynolds, Michigan, a dozen farmers saw an airship land in a field and then found inside it a 9-foot-tall humanoid. The *Saginaw Courier-Herald* reported that the being seemed to try to communicate with the onlookers, but his speech sounded like "bellowing."

Near Cassville, Indiana, airship occupants were described as "foreign-tongued midgets who spoke no English" in a May 3rd sighting. Also, a pilot who was "clearly not an inhabitant of this world" was recovered from the wreckage of an airship crash on April 17, in Aurora, Texas, as we will discuss in our next chapter.

By around the first week of June 1897, the wave of airship sightings seemed to just stop. Very few were reported after that. The many newspaper articles from 1897 confirm that something really strange did happen. Unfortunately, we may never know exactly what.

CHAPTER 13

ALIEN BODY RECOVERED IN NORTH TEXAS (1897)

In a previous chapter, we described the explosion of a UFO over a cotton gin in Dublin, Texas in 1891. Six years later, in 1897, another very strange incident took place about 100 miles away. It happened in the tiny town of Aurora, Texas on Saturday, April 17, 1897 at 6 o'clock in the morning.

A cigar-shaped UFO, metallic silver in color, appeared suddenly in the sky above Aurora. It was moving from south to north. Unlike the balloon airships of its time, this UFO was built of "an unknown metal, resembling somewhat a mix of aluminum and silver." A witness guessed that the ship weighed "several tons."

The sighting occurred during a time when many strange airships were being seen all over the United States. For this reason, the UFO is called an "airship" in a newspaper article written later by Aurora resident S. E. Haydon.

Haydon told the *Dallas Morning News* that the strange craft seemed to be having some kind of mechanical problems. It slowed down to about ten or twelve miles per hour and began settling toward the ground.

Haydon said the townspeople watched in amazement as the slow-moving airship drifted over the town square and then moved north toward the property of Judge J. S. Proctor. Next, the UFO collided with a windmill on the judge's land and "went into pieces with a terrific explosion, scattering debris over several acres of ground." The crash destroyed the windmill, the adjacent water tank and the judge's flower garden.

It seems likely that the explosion and crash drew many spectators to Judge Proctor's land. Among the wreckage, the townspeople found the dead body of the ship's pilot. Then the story got really weird. Witnesses said the pilot was not human.

Haydon said that, although the pilot's body was damaged severely in the crash, it was clear that "he was not an inhabitant of this world." The pilot may have been from Mars, said another witness, Mr. T. J. Weems, an officer in the U.S. Signal Service and an "authority on astronomy."

In the case of the UFO that exploded in 1891 over

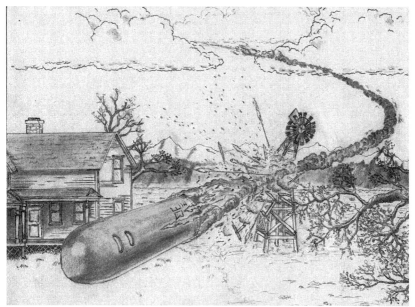

Cigar-shaped UFO Strikes Windmill (Illustration by Neil Riebe)

Dublin, Texas, papers were found containing strange writing on them. The same thing happened in Aurora. When the townspeople checked the pilot's body, they found that he was carrying papers written in an unknown language. The papers may have contained a record of the pilot's journeys, but they were "written in some unknown hieroglyphics" and could not be understood.

As word of what happened reached surrounding towns, many visitors arrived to look at the crash site. Haydon commented, "The town is full of people today who are viewing the wreck and gathering specimens of the strange metal from the debris." It's possible that some of that mysterious wreckage that was carried away from Aurora still exists today, stored away and forgotten in attics or storage rooms. None of it has ever

A Windmill Demolishes It.

Aurora, Wise Co., Tex., April 17.—(To The News.)—About 6 o'clock this morning the early risers of Aurora were astonished at the sudden appearance of the airship which has been sailing through the country.

It was traveling due north, and much nearer the earth than ever before. Evidently some of the machinery was out of order, for it was making a speed of only ten or twelve miles an hour and gradually settling toward the earth. It sailed directly over the public square, and when it reached the north part of town collided with the tower of Judge Proctor's windmill and went to pieces with a terrific explosion, scattering debris over several acres of ground, wrecking the windmill and water tank and destroying the judge's flower garden.

The pilot of the ship is supposed to have been the only one on board, and while his remains are badly disfigured, enough of the original has been picked up to show that he was not an inhabitant of this world.

Mr. T. J. Weems, the United States signal service officer at this place and an authority on astronomy, gives it as his opinion that he was a native of the planet Mars.

Papers found on his person—evidently the record of his travels—are written in some unknown hieroglyphics, and can not be deciphered.

The ship was too badly wrecked to form any conclusion as to its construction or motive power. It was built of an unknown metal, resembling somewhat a mixture of aluminum and silver, and it must have weighed several tons.

The town is full of people to-day who are viewing the wreck and gathering specimens of the strange metal from the debris. The pilot's funeral will take place at noon to-morrow. S. E. HAYDON.

Actual Newspaper Article from Dallas Morning News, 4-19-1897

been found, though.

After the crash, the townspeople tried to find out more about how the UFO was constructed and what made it fly. However, Haydon said that the ship was "too badly wrecked to form any conclusion as to its construction or motive power."

The *Dallas Morning News* article, published two days after the crash, said that the pilot's funeral would take place on April 18. Another newspaper, The *Fort Worth Register*, said, "The pilot, who was not an inhabitant of this world, was given proper Christian burial at the Aurora Cemetery."

When the pilot was buried, a marker was placed on his grave. In 1973, newspaper reporter Bill Case described the marker as having a strange design on it resembling a flying saucer with portholes. Shortly after Case wrote a story describing the grave marker, somebody stole it. Today, nobody is sure exactly where the pilot was buried.

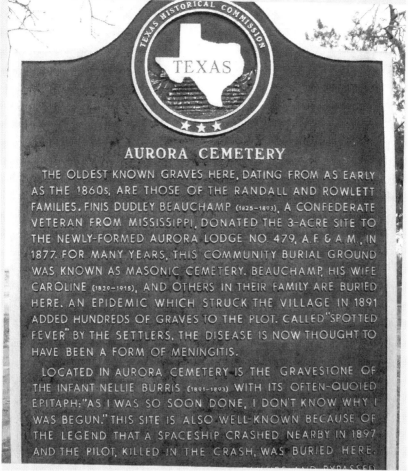

State Historical Marker at Aurora Cemetery (Photo by Noe Torres)

In 2008, an unmarked grave dating back to the 1890s was found at the Aurora Cemetery during the filming of a television show called "UFO Hunters" for the *History Channel*. Since the owners of the cemetery will not allow anyone to dig up the grave, nobody knows if it is the grave of the strange pilot.

Although some people claim the story is not true and was created by Aurora residents to boost tourism, many other people to believe that a spaceship crash-landed there. In fact, the state's historical commission has placed a permanent marker at the cemetery that mentions the spaceship crash. The marker says,

"This site is also well-known because of the legend that a spaceship crashed nearby in 1897 and the pilot, killed in the crash, was buried here."

The case of the alien that fell from the sky in Aurora, Texas, continues to fascinate people to this very day. It has been featured on many television documentaries and in many books. The Aurora UFO crash still remains as much of a mystery today as it was back in 1897.

CHAPTER 14

ALIEN CATTLE RUSTLERS (1897)

Beginning in the 1970s cows were mysteriously being found dead on ranches all across New Mexico and
the Southwest. Investigators sent out to determine their
cause of death were baffled. From what they could tell,
the cows weren't killed by animals, but instead some
form of intelligent life using surgical tools to remove

85

various organs from inside the cows. It didn't take long for people to theorize that aliens were the ones behind this new phenomenon.

It's an easy scenario to imagine: a lonely cow grazes alone in the darkness. A light soon appears in the sky and hovers over the poor cow. Soon a light shines down onto the animal and lifts it up into the ship to befall its terrible fate.

There is actually an account of cattle abduction back in the Old West. And it is humorously primitive compared to modern cattle abduction premises.

The story first appeared in the April 23, 1897 edition of the *Yates Center Farmer's Advocate*, a Kansas based newspaper. It was late at night when Alex Hamilton, a Leroy, Kansas, rancher awoke to a strange noise coming from outside. His cattle sounded as if something were scaring them badly. Hamilton ran to the door and could see an airship slowly approaching his cattle from the air.

According to Hamilton the airship was cigar-shaped and had a carriage underneath it. The carriage he said looked to be made of glass and was illuminated within. Inside of it were "three of the strangest beings" Hamilton had ever seen, two men, a woman, and three children. However, what made these beings so strange Hamilton never elaborated on.

Hamilton called his son Wall and another man that lived on the ranch, Gid Heslip, for assistance. The three men grabbed some axes and ran for the corral. As they ran closer to the airship they could hear the "beings" talking in a strange language which they could not understand.

86

Photo Courtesy of T. Voekler & Wikipedia

The strange craft then shone a bright spotlight on the group and got closer. It was then that the three men noticed a poor calf with a cable around its neck being hauled up into the airship. For the moment, the poor calf seemed to be caught in the fence, so the trio of men bravely tried to cut her loose. But it was no use. They could not cut the cable and watched helplessly as the airship drifted away from them taking the poor calf with them.

The next day Lank Thomas, who lived several miles from the Hamilton farm, found the calf's butchered remains on his property. There were no tracks around it, so it was if it had been lowered or dropped to the ground from the air.

Soon the newspapers picked up on the story and created quite a stir. There was even an affidavit issued attesting to Hamilton's honesty, which said:

"As there are now, always have been, and always will be skeptics and unbelievers, whenever the truth of anything bordering on the improbable is presented, and knowing that some ignorant or superstitious people will doubt the truthfulness of the above account, now, therefore, we, the undersigned, do hereby make the following affidavit. That we have known Alex Hamilton from fifteen to thirty years and that for truth and veracity have never heard his word questioned and that we do verily believe his statement to be true and correct."

The *Yates Center Farmer's Advocate* said, "Mr. Hamilton looked as if he had not entirely recovered from the shock and everyone who knew him was convinced he was sincere in every word."

However, in the 1940s, the truth about the story came out. You see, Hamilton was part of something called a Liar's Club. A Liar's Club was a group of men who went about telling tall tales and seeing who could outdo one another. Well, Hamilton out did them all. So much so that the Liar's Club broke up after his story went public. Actually, it is possible that fellow members of the Liar's Club were the ones to sign the affidavit attesting to Hamilton's truthfulness.

The truth came out in 1943 in an old Kansas newspaper, the *Enterprise*. In it, the editor of the *Yates Center Farmer's Advocate*, F. Hudson, came clean and admitted knowing that Hamilton's airship story was a fake all the way back when he published it! And how did Hudson know this? He was with his friend Hamilton when he made up the story.

But what inspired Hamilton to make up such a strange story? The previous year, 1896, had been the year of the great airship wave, with newspapers reporting on the mystery craft often. Also, back in the Old West there was something called cattle rustling. To rustle cattle a thief would come along, steal someone's cattle, change the cattle's brand (the marks that showed who it belonged to) to something else, and then sell it. Most likely Hamilton thought it would be funny to have one of the famous airships "rustle" his cattle.

There also exists a similar story that pre-dates this one. It supposedly occurred in 1896 and took place on a farm in Howell County, Missouri. The story was told by an old woman, Pearl Chenoweth, to the Missouri Historical Society before she died in 1984. At the time of her UFO sighting in 1896, Pearl was a young girl who along with her brother Ben saw a bright circle of lights "swirling" around in the air. The two siblings ran to get their parents and together they all watched the saucer like object hover over the family barn with a blinding light.

The family ran to their living room in fear where they prayed for safety. Later, Pearl's father got up to go look outside and the craft was gone. The next day the family went out to investigate the spot where the UFO had been hovering. They were shocked to find burnt grass and three dead steers.

They described the dead steers as, "completely drained of blood. The only marks on them were some dried blood on their throats from two puncture holes in the jugular vein; these looked as though they had been made by a two-tined fork..."

Pearl Chenoweth continued to relate how the newspaper from St. Louis related several similar stories all happening on the same night across Missouri. In each case a bright circle of light hovered over the cattle, and no matter how many cattle there were to take the next morning only three were found on each ranch dead, all drained of blood just like the cows found by Pearl and her family. Some speculated whatever was killing the cattle were blood-sucking extraterrestrials. In other words, alien vampires.

However, researchers today have never been able to find the newspapers that Mrs. Chenoweth described. This leads some to say that she got her dates wrong, and therefore that specific newspaper issue is harder to find. Others actually think Mrs. Chenoweth's story was inspired by the made up by Alex Hamilton. After all, it was 1897 when Hamilton's story was published in newspapers across the country, including ones in Missouri. Perhaps Mrs. Chenoweth got her date wrong and actually meant 1897. On the other hand, even if she did read Hamilton's story in the newspaper, why would she then make up a story that she herself had seen a UFO? It is a confusing matter for certain.

And as for Hamilton, even though his story was proven to be a hoax, isn't it an even odder coincidence that later in the 20th Century, many cattle really were mutilated, possibly by extraterrestrials, all across the world?

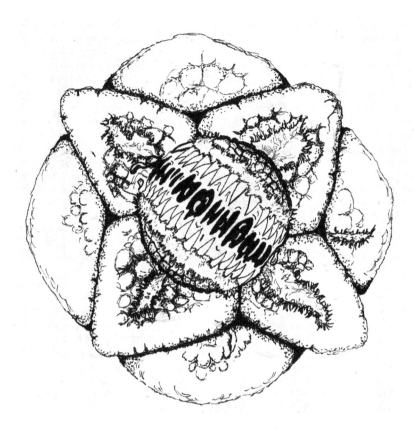

AFTERWORD
THE CACTUS THAT ATE THE WORLD

It was a sunny day in Las Cruces, New Mexico, and Pat Garrett was having a big argument. Some of you may remember the name Pat Garrett. He was the Sheriff who in 1891 shot and killed the Old West's most notorious outlaw, 21-year-old Billy the Kid.

The year was now 1908, almost thirty years after Garrett killed the Kid, and Garrett was having a squabble with another 21-year-old, Jesse Wayne Brazel. Garrett was angry because Brazel had driven goats onto Garrett's land, and the goats were eating his grass.

This may not sound like a fantastic story now, but would you find it more interesting to know that this argument had been planned out by a group of conspirators who wanted Pat Garrett dead? One of the conspirators was even a well-known lawyer, who some said was the most powerful man in Southern New Mexico, Albert Bacon Fall.

You see, several months earlier Fall and his fellow conspirators had gotten together to discuss a way to get rid of Garrett, the once famous lawman. To do so they called in an Old West assassin by the name of "Killer" Jim Miller. Miller agreed to kill Garrett for $5,000, just as long as it never got blamed on him.

This is where Jesse Wayne Brazel and his goats came in. The goats running loose on Garrett's land was merely an excuse to get Garrett out in the open on a lonely road nearby his land. There in the distance, while Brazel and Garrett argued about the goats, Miller, the hired assassin, waited with his rifle at a safe distance.

At the right moment, Miller fired, killing the famous lawman. Jesse Brazel then went into town to see the sheriff. There, he claimed that he had shot Garrett in self-defense when Garrett became violent. Brazel even had a witness, Carl Adamson, who lied on Brazel's behalf, claiming that Brazel shot Garrett in self-defense.

The Old West conspiracy worked. Brazel went free and so did "Killer" Miller, the real assassin. At least

Rancher W.W. "Mack" Brazel in 1947 (Courtesy of HSSNM and the Roswell Daily Record)

that's how the legend goes. As with any good story, there are several different versions.

But, you may ask, what does this story have to do with UFOs? Well, we'll get to that, too. In the year 1947, the term flying saucer was finally adopted to describe UFOs. No longer were mysterious things in the air called "airships" or "flying dragons." This happened after a man named Kenneth Arnold saw several flying saucers from out his window while he was flying an airplane. His sighting became a media sensation. Now just about everyone knew what UFOs and flying saucers were.

People all over the country began to see them.

Newspapers even began offering rewards for proof of one. Eventually one man did find proof. His name was William "Mack" Brazel, a cousin of Jesse Wayne

94

Brazel. Like his cousin, Mack would become involved in one of the greatest conspiracies of all time, The Roswell Incident, which is widely recognized as the world's most famous UFO case.

Mack Brazel was a cowboy who watched over a sheep ranch near a little town called Corona, about 75 miles northwest of Roswell, New Mexico. Mack was born in 1899, just as the Old West was coming to an end. By 1947, when this story happened he was about 48 years old. On a stormy July night in 1947 Mack heard an explosion in the sky that wasn't thunder. The next day, his ranch was covered in strange metallic wreckage. What made it so strange was that when you crumpled the thin metal up in your hand, it would unfold perfectly smooth without even a wrinkle!

But that's not all that Mack found. At another site were the bodies of strange beings. They were short, grey-skinned, and had large heads and eyes. It was as if an alien craft had exploded over his ranch dumping out the wreckage and the bodies.

Not knowing what to do, Mack took samples of the wreckage to Roswell, the nearest big city. It was a decision Mack would regret. Soon the military found out about Mack and his wreckage. Instead of treating him like a hero, the military took Mack into custody and held him prisoner for over a week!

Most people today believe that an alien craft exploded over Mack's ranch, and then the rest of the craft crashed at a location closer to Roswell. Each year, thousands of visitors from all over the world go to Roswell to commemorate the UFO crash. However, the military claimed that what crashed there in 1947 was just a weather balloon. In order to cover up the UFO crash, the military persuaded Mack Brazel change his original story and tell people that what he found on his ranch was really just a balloon.

Before the military talked to him, Mack claimed what he found was pieces of a flying saucer and alien bodies. After the military took him into custody and held him for a week under intense interrogation, he apparently agreed to tell the military's version of the story.

This was known as the great cover-up. For a time, it worked and people really did think it was a weather balloon after all, but later, in the 1970s, people began to doubt that story when many eyewitnesses started coming forward and giving testimony about what they saw in Roswell in 1947.

As for Mack, the military eventually let him go, but he was never the same after. The town of Roswell, on the other hand, now considers the UFO crash, whether its real or not, to be the best thing that ever happened to it. Every year in July people gather in Roswell to celebrate a UFO Festival, and the town is now known as the UFO Capital of the World.

Because it is now associated with all things alien, Roswell occasionally has some very strange things happen there even today. For instance, a few years ago a strange rock was found outside of Roswell. What made it so strange was that it had a crop-circle engraved on it that matches a crop-circle found all the way in England! Also adding to the rock's mystery is the fact that when put under a magnet it would spin round and round.

More recently, KRQE news reported on an even stranger find in Roswell-the alien cactus. David Salman, a scientist who studies plants, was collecting seeds outside of Roswell in the spring of 2010 when he noticed a faint glow coming from an old meteor crater. Inching closer to the crater, the botanist discovered that the eerie glow was coming from a group of nearly 1,000 small cacti (that's plural for cactus)!

What's more, the botanist went on to speculate that the strange cacti might have come on the meteor and possibly are carnivorous, just like a Venus Fly Trap. Another theory put forth by the botanist was maybe the cacti came to earth as seeds or spores on the meteor that scattered upon impact.

On a return visit to the crater, Salman said the cacti had spread out and multiplied, moving away from the crater. How soon might they come to your town? Probably never.

You see, even though Salman claims to have found these cacti in 2010, he didn't release the story until April Fool's Day, 2011. "The cactus that ate the world," Albuquerque newsman Dick Knipfing said jokingly. Well put, Mr. Knipfing, well put.

Like many of the incredible tales we've heard about UFO encounters in the Old West, we remain uncertain whether they are true or were merely the equivalent of somebody's strange April Fool's joke.

ABOUT THE ARTISTS

We would like to acknowledge the gifted artists who made outstanding contributions to this book. The artist whose illustrations appear at the start of each chapter, Neil Riebe, is an author and illustrator living in Madison, Wisconsin. He has written articles and short stories for *G-Fan Magazine, Prehistoric Times, Goldenvisions, Sounds of the Night,*  *Japanese Giants of Filmland* and several short story anthologies. His illustrations appear in *Towns of Lincoln County* by Arcadia Publishing, several role playing games, and *Roswell, USA: Towns That Celebrate UFOs, Lake Monsters, Bigfoot and Other Weirdness.* He can be contacted at neilriebe@yahoo.com or just search "Neil Riebe" on Facebook.com.

Shane Olive, who did the front cover artwork, is a retired firefighter living in Roswell, New Mexico. He has worked in illustrating for over 30 years. His past works include book covers, VHS box art, and illustrations for various magazines, including *TV Guide.*

Jared Olive, who also contributed several illustrations for this book, is the son of Shane Olive and is a firefighter in Roswell. He has designed t-shirts and logos for products sold in Roswell gift shops, but this is his first major illustrative work.

BIBLIOGRAPHY

"An Electric Monster." *The Devil's Penny Harbringer.* www.devilspenny.com/2009/06/an-electric-monster-1893/

Booth, B. J. "January 1878, Denison, Texas, Daylight UFO." *UFO Casebook.* www.ufocasebook.com/denisontexas1878.html

Brueske, Judith M. *The Marfa Lights.* Alpine, TX: Ocotillo Enterprises, 1991.

Childress, David H. "Living Pterodactyls." *Far-Out Adventures: The Best of World Explorer.* Kempton, IL: Adventures Unlimited, 2001.

Clark, Jerome. *Extraordinary Encounters: An Encyclopedia of Extraterrestrials and Otherworldly Beings.* Santa Barbara, CA: ABC-CLIO, 2000.

Clark, Jerome. *The UFO Encyclopedia, 2nd Edition.* Detroit, MI: Omnigraphics, Inc., 1998.

Clarke, Jerome and Nancy Pear. *Strange & Unexplained Happenings: When Nature Breaks the Rules of Science.* New York:UXL, 1995.

Cohen, Daniel. *The Great Airship Mystery: A UFO of the 1890s*. New York: Dodd, Mead, & Company, 1981.

Cox, Mike and Renee Roderick. *Texas UFO Tales: From Denison 1878 to Stephenville 2008*. Dallas: Atriad Press LLC, 2009.

Dennett, Preston. *UFOS Over California: A True History of Extraterrestrials in the Golden State*. Atglen, PA: Schiffer Publishing, 2005.

Edwards, Frank. *Flying Saucers - Serious Business*. New York: Lyle Stuart, 1966.

Hall, Mark A. *Thunderbirds: America's Living Legends of Giant Birds*. New York: Paraview Press, 2004.

Heinselman, Craig. "Thunderbird." Cryptozoology.com. www.cryptozoology.com/cryptids/thunderbird.php.

Keel, John A. *The Complete Guide to Mysterious Beings*. New York: Tor, 2002.

Menzel, Donald H. and Ernest H. Taves. *The UFO Enigma: The Definitive Explanation of the UFO Phenomenon*. New York: Doubleday & Company, Inc., 1977.

Murphy, Mark and Noe Torres. "UFO Crash in North Texas, 1891." BeyondBoundaries.org. www.beyondboundaries.org.

"Nebraska Cowboys Witness Spectacular UFO Crash in 1887." Rense.com. www.rense.com/general74/visitor.htm.

"Nebraska May Have Had Its Own Roswell in 1884." *The Daily Nebraskan*. July 13, 2008. www.dailynebraskan.com/a-e/nebraska-may-have-had-its-own-roswell-in-1884-1.284477

Randles, Jenny and Peter Hough. *The Complete Book of UFOS: An Investigation into Alien Contacts & Encounters*. New York: Sterling Publishing, 1994.

Rickard, Bob and John Mitchell. *Unexplained Phenomena: A Rough Guide Special*. London: Rough Guides Ltd., 2000.

"Sightings of Marfa Lights in Texas." *Live Pterosaur Blog Site*. http://www.livepterosaur.com/LP_Blog/archives/858

Steiger, Brad. "Crazy Bears and UFOs." *Alien Seeker News*. www.alienseekernews.com/articles/crazy-bears-ufos.html.

"The Mysterious Thunderbird Photo." *PrarieGhosts.com*. www.prairieghosts.com/tbirdaz.html

"Thunderbird." *Parascope.com.*
www.parascope.com/en/cryptozoo/predators10.h
tm

Wikipedia contributors. "Aurora, Texas UFO incident."
Wikipedia, The Free Encyclopedia. Wikipedia,
The Free Encyclopedia.

Wood, Ryan S. *Majic Eyes Only: Earth's Encounters
With Extraterrestrial Technology.* Broomfield,
CO: Wood Enterprises, 2005.

INDEX

Also Available From RoswellBooks:
Order at Amazon.com or RoswellBooks.com
Kindle Edition Available.

An Inside Look at the Roswell UFO
Festival and Other Weird Celebrations.

The Amazing Story of a UFO Crash
near Del Rio, Texas in 1955.

The Other Roswell

UFO Crash on the Texas-Mexico Border

Noe Torres and Ruben Uriarte

As Told to the Authors By
Colonel Robert B. Willingham,
U.S. Air Force Reserve (Ret.)

Read the Book that Spawned Two Major
TV Documentaries. The Story of a UFO
Encounter near Presidio, Texas in 1974.

Mexico's Roswell

The Chihuahua UFO Crash

Second Edition

By Noe Torres
and Ruben Uriarte

*As Featured on the
History Channel's
"UFO Hunters" and "UFO Files"*

Afterword by Stanton T. Friedman

Made in the USA
Charleston, SC
29 June 2012